EARLY LEARN TOGETHER SERIES

FIRST SKILLS PLAYBOOK

Walter's Bazaar

RICHARD DAWSON

A Piccolo Original
Piccolo Books

This series has been prepared in consultation with the Pre-school Playgroups Association.

Can you find two of everything in Walter's shop?

- Everything starts with 't'. Can you think of other things beginning with 't'?
- Talk about junk shops, how some old things are valuable, some are not so.
- Play 'hunt the spider'.

Which keys did Walter press to write his name?

Matching

WALTER

- Which letters would you press for your name ?
- Talk about keyboards of typewriters being the same as computer keyboards.
- Point out the difference between higher/lower case letters and the fact that keyboards are usually 'big' letters.
- Encourage your child to use 'small' letters when he/she starts to write, except for the first letter of names.

What can Walter see through his telescope?

- Talk about up/down, far away/near, bigger/smaller. Look at things further away and nearer, and bigger and smaller than yourself.
- Talk about the sorts of people who might use telescopes.

Can you see what Walter is looking at high up in the sky?

● Talk about the comparatives: high, higher, highest.

Can you find the odd umbrella in each row?

- Put an odd sock in with a pair and pick out the odd one.
- Mix up some cutlery, e.g. five identical dessert spoons and a soup spoon and pick out the odd one. Count the umbrellas in each row.

Which umbrella will each customer choose?

- Mix up clothes and pick out those that could be worn together.
- Look at the decoration around the house and see how paints, papers and furniture match.

Can you find the violins that are the same on each shelf?

- Talk about musical instruments and the sounds they make.
- Play some records or cassettes of violin music.
- Mix up some some pairs with an odd one e.g. shoes. If possible make the odd one similar and then sort them out. Count the violins in each row.

Which violin fits Walter's case?

- Which bow goes with which violin?
- Mix up family shoes and then identify them by their size.

Can you find Walter's van?

NO
WAITING

- Who do you think the other vans might belong to?
- Talk about signs in the street and how they can be used to find things out e.g. No Waiting sign picture.

Which clocks show the same time as Walter's watch?

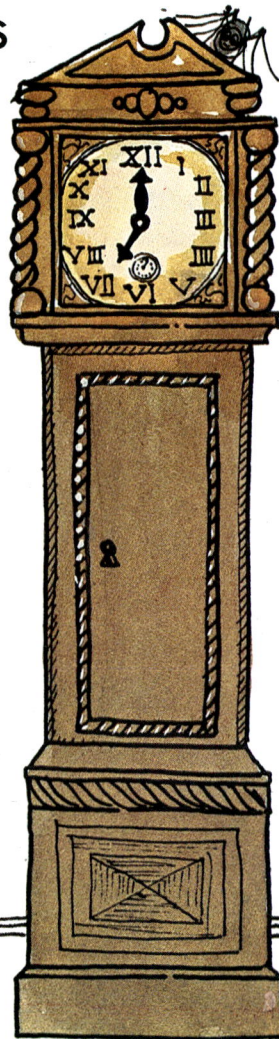

- Look at the clocks around the house, central heating clock, cooker, video clock, etc. Look at differences between clocks, i.e. analogue and digital.
- Talk about the clocks in Walter's shop. See if the child can recognize the numbers on the clock faces.
- Talk about telling the time concentrating on the 'o' clocks.
- Count the clocks in the shop.

Where have Walter's wheels come from?

• Count all the things with wheels in your house. Look at different kinds and discuss the different jobs wheels do.

Can you find Walter's other boot?

- Sort out other pairs of boots in the picture. Notice the one odd boot.
- Mixed shoes, gloves or socks could be sorted by children.

Which coat will Walter choose?

- Discuss what the weather is like outside. What job do you think Walter is going to do?
- Look out for local weather vanes. Why did people have and use them?

Which fox fits in which box?

- Count the foxes and count the boxes.
- Games can be played fitting things back into the correct box e.g. toy car into its box. Introduce different size boxes and see which box the car will fit in.
- See how many objects you can fit into a matchbox.
- When in the bath use different size vessels, cup, mug, jug, etc. and transfer water from one to the other.

Which yo-yo is Walter holding?

- Ask the child to pick the yo-yo without finger tracing. Check to see if correct by finger tracing.

Can you find each yacht's sails?

Can you pick out all the toy zoo animals?

- Talk about zoo animals being wild animals that have been captured, and farm animals being domesticated animals.
- Mix up any small toys that you have and sort them out, e.g. mixed up cars could be sorted to sets of lorries, vans, cars; stuffed toys into bears, dogs, etc.

Can you follow the stripes Walter is painting on the zebra?

a is for apple all rosy and red,
b is for bear who sleeps on the bed,
c is for cat which catches the mice,
d is for dog all cuddly and nice,
e is for egg, Walter has for his tea,
f is for fire to warm you and me,
g is for goat Walter keeps in the shed,
h is for hat that fits on your head,
i is for insects that all have six legs,
j is for jackets that hang on the pegs,
k is for kites that fly in the sky,
l is for ladder that takes you up high,
m is for mouse that's escaped from the cat,
n is for net to catch fish big and fat,
o is for orange that Walter is peeling,
p is for parrot that swings from the ceiling,
q is for quilt that's all warm and soft,
r is for rat that lives in the loft,
s is for spider you'll find in this book,
t is for telephone left off the hook,
u is for umbrella to keep off the rain,
v is for Walter's old weather vane,
w is for wellingtons worn in the wet
x is in fox that's not usually a pet,
y is for yacht that sails on the sea,
z is for zebra that ends A B C.

- Look for all the objects in Walter's shop.
- Use the letter sound rather than the alphabet name.

Early reading, writing and number skills in this book

Left to right movement

To read and write, we have to move our eyes and hand from left to right. As this doesn't come naturally, plenty of practice is needed: finger tracing, tracing with a pencil, noting that we start on the left when reading, etc. All the pages of this book are designed with the focal point on the left-hand side of the page.

Pattern practice/ hand control/ coordination

The patterns for the children to trace with their fingers practise the curved and straight lines which will be needed when writing proper begins, and also help develop the necessary hand control and hand-eye coordination. Scribbling, colouring, mazes, painting, cutting, sticking, playing with Lego are some other activities which develop these skills.

Counting/number value/one-to-one correspondence

As well as learning to chant the numbers in order, children need to understand what each number actually represents (i.e. two = two things etc.) and that each object being counted is only counted once. Musical chairs (without removing a chair), laying the table (giving each person a knife, fork, etc.), and taking every opportunity to count around the house will all help.

Discrimination (sorting, matching, pairs, odd one out position)

Sorting and matching, noticing and describing how things are the same and how they are different—patterns, colours, shapes, sizes,—are all important for reading, writing and number work. Jigsaw puzzles, lotto, dominoes and numerous other games and activities around the house are all useful practice for these skills.

Prediction

Connecting an experience with its likely outcome will help with reading and writing—guessing word and letter order and imagining what will happen in a story so that reading makes sense. Try predicting what is going to happen on the next page of a story you are reading.

Rhyme

Because rhymes, particularly traditional nursery rhymes, are so easy to learn by heart children can 'pretend' to read them. This is not cheating, but an important first step to reading and should be encouraged. Many of the traditional rhymes also include actions to help with counting.

Letter sounds

These will help with the later stages of learning to read when unknown words can be built up by their sounds. (The letter names—the alphabet, ABC—do not help with reading.) The sounds should be made with as little voice as possible. Playing I-Spy using the letter sounds is fun, but don't worry if it takes a while before the connection between the word and its letter sound is developed. If necessary, try the game later.